YEARNING FOR LEARNING
THE ADVENTURES OF K

PUBLISHED BY TIMELESS LIFESKILLS LIMITED
COPYRIGHT © 2014 ALL RIGHTS RESERVED
ISBN 978-1-908102-10-2

WORDS: POOJA PANDE

ART: DOLPH VAN EDEN

AUTHOR'S PREFACE

THAT FIRST SPARK FOR LEARNING — TRUE LEARNING — THE KIND THAT ALMOST CAUGHT YOU UNAWARES, INSTIGATED IN YOU THE DESIRE TO REALLY UNDERSTAND SOMETHING, TO LEARN SOMETHING NEW, FOR YOUR OWN SELF ONLY AND FOR NO OTHER REASON (BETTER GRADES, LEAVING AN IMPRESSION ON SOMEBODY, ADMISSION TO A RENOWNED INSTITUTE), AND LEFT YOU AN ALTERED PERSON, IS A STORY WITH AS MANY VERSIONS AS THERE ARE PEOPLE.

IF YOU THINK BACK, THERE WOULD HAVE BEEN SEVERAL PEOPLE WHO INSPIRED YOU ALONG THE WAY - A FATHER WHO PLANNED NATURE WALKS, A MOTHER WHO READ BOOKS, A SCHOOL TEACHER WHO LEFT IT TO YOU TO MAKE YOUR OWN CLASSROOM AGENDA ONCE A MONTH, A KNOW-IT-ALL UNCLE WHO REGALED YOU WITH FASCINATING TRAVEL STORIES - BUT THEY WERE, IN THE END, EXACTLY JUST THAT - THOSE WHO INSPIRED YOU TO EMBARK ON A LIFETIME OF LEARNING, AND HELPED YOU WITH IT - FACILITATORS.

THE MOST POWERFUL MOMENTS OF LEARNING — TRUE LEARNING — WOULD BE THE ONES WHERE YOU RECOGNIZED THE URGE, THE FIRE INSIDE YOU AND WENT ABOUT CHARTING YOUR OWN PATH. THE TEACHERS IN YOUR JOURNEY (AND TODAY, THIS INCLUDES TECHNOLOGY AS AN ENABLING FACTOR) ACTING AS GUIDING LIGHTS — ILLUMINATING YOUR WAY. THAT DRIVE THOUGH, IS ALL YOU. AS IS THE JOY YOU GAIN FROM IT.

OUR ATTEMPT WITH THIS BOOK IS TO TALK ABOUT THE JOURNEY OF LEARNING WE ALL UNDERTAKE AND HOW WE CAN NURTURE AND CHERISH IT (BECAUSE EVEN AS IT STARTS YOUNG, IT FIZZLES OUT ONLY TOO SOON), MAKE IT GROW SUCH THAT WE ALL LEARN FOR THE SAKE OF LEARNING, FOR JOY, FOR OUR OWN SELVES.

— POOJA PANDE

FOREWORD

FORMAL EDUCATION TENDS TO BEHAVE LIKE A GPS GIVING LEARNERS STEP-BY-STEP INSTRUCTIONS FOR A WELL-DEFINED WORLD. THIS GPS APPROACH WORKED WELL IN THE 19TH AND 20TH CENTURIES WHEN STOCKPILING KNOWLEDGE IN A DOMAIN, IN THE FORM OF A UNIVERSITY DEGREE, USUALLY ASSURED LIFELONG EMPLOYMENT BECAUSE RATE OF KNOWLEDGE ACCUMULATION IN MOST DOMAINS WAS NOT VERY HIGH.

IN THE 21ST CENTURY, KNOWLEDGE IS EXPLODING AND THE MAP IS CHANGING EVERY MINUTE. WHEN THE TERRAIN IS CHANGING SO FAST, NO GPS CAN HELP. LEARNERS NEED A COMPASS. AN INNER COMPASS THAT ENCOURAGES LEARNERS TO THINK FOR THEMSELVES. ONE THAT MAKES THEM INTROSPECT IF THEY SHOULD LEARN ONLY TO EARN? OR ASK - WHY EARN, Y-EARN SO THAT THEY FIRST YEARN TO LEARN, EVEN AS THEY EARN AND CONTINUE LEARNING UNTIL THEY ARE IN THE URN!

CHANCES ARE THAT LEARNERS TODAY WILL CHANGE MANY CAREERS IN THEIR LIFETIME AND FORMAL EDUCATION AT BEST PREPARES THEM FOR THEIR FIRST CAREER. TO THRIVE AND SHINE, THEY WILL NEED TO CONSTANTLY LEARN AND REINVENT THEMSELVES.

FOR THIS, THEY WILL HAVE TO LEARN THE ART AND SCIENCE OF SELF-DIRECTED LEARNING AND BECOME DEEPLY SELF-AWARE ABOUT DISPOSITIONS LIKE INTRINSIC MOTIVATION, EMOTIONAL RESILIENCE, DELAYED GRATIFICATION, GROWTH MINDSET, GRIT AND ABILITY TO FACE FAILURE AND RIDICULE.

IN THIS COMIC BOOK, OUR 15-YEAR OLD HERO TAKES A DEEP DIVE INTO UNDERSTANDING SELF-DIRECTED LEARNING SKILLS AND FINDS OUT HOW HE CAN INSPIRE HIMSELF TO YEARN TO LEARN AND MAKING THE MOST OF ONLINE RESOURCES, CRAFT LEARNING EXPERIENCES THAT ARE FUN FOR HIM. HE DISCOVERS HIS PASSION AND EMPOWERS HIMSELF TO PURSUE IT WITH COMPASSION.

THIS IS OUR HOPE AND DESIRE FOR ALL THOSE WHO TURN THE PAGE...

- ATUL PANT
FOUNDER, TIMELESS LIFESKILLS

MEET K

A 15-YEAR-OLD BOY, WHO GOES TO SCHOOL FOR THE BETTER PART OF THE DAY, SEMI-RELUCTANTLY.

HIS ROOM IS HIS MAIN PAD, A STATE OF BEING, AS FAR AS HE'S CONCERNED – A PLACE UNVISITED BY FAMILY (HIS NEXT DOOR NEIGHBOURS) FOR DAYS ON END. IT'S HOW HE LIKES IT.

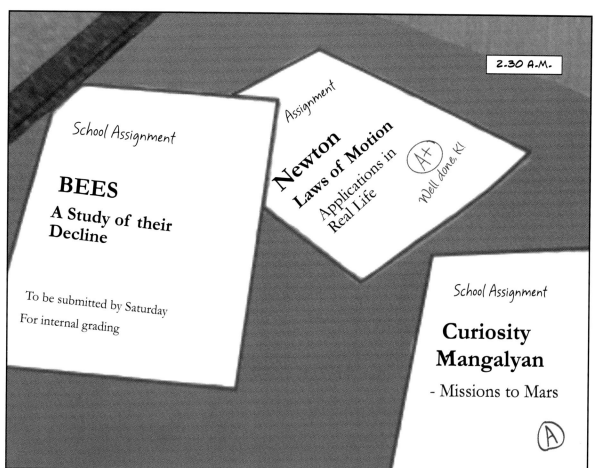

K. HEY. WAKE UP.'

HUH!

GET UP.

WHAT! WHO ARE YOU?

WHAT ARE YOU DOING IN MY ROOM? WHAT TIME IS IT?

WHAT'S THAT YOU'RE WEARING? WHAT'S WITH THE BOB MARLEY LOOK?

WAKE UP, K. I HAVE SOMETHING IMPORTANT TO TELL YOU. MY NAME IS EKLAVYA. BUT YOU CAN CALL ME EK.

WHAT DO YOU HAVE TO TELL ME? ARE YOU FROM AROUND HERE? DO YOU GO TO MY SCHOOL? EK?

NO, I'M NOT FROM AROUND HERE. AND NO, I DON'T GO TO SCHOOL,

IT CRAMPED MY STYLE. SO, I NEVER DID.

THE MAGIC WORDS! K IS NOW FULLY AWAKE.

WE LIVED IN THE FOREST, MY CLAN AND I.

"WE ALL HAD OUR DUTIES ASSIGNED TO US. MINE WAS WEAPONRY - I WOULD SPEND HOURS CRAFTING THE PERFECT BOW FROM WOOD."

"CHOOSING THE RIGHT TWIGS, THE BARK OF THE TREE FOR MY ARROWS."

"IT WASN'T JUST MY PASSION, I WOULD LOSE MYSELF IN IT."

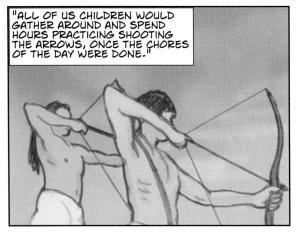

"ALL OF US CHILDREN WOULD GATHER AROUND AND SPEND HOURS PRACTICING SHOOTING THE ARROWS, ONCE THE CHORES OF THE DAY WERE DONE."

AIM FOR THAT MANGO THERE. THAT ONE LOOKS RIPE-OVER THERE! EKLAVYA, SHOOT

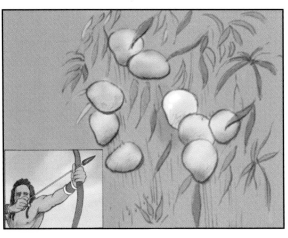

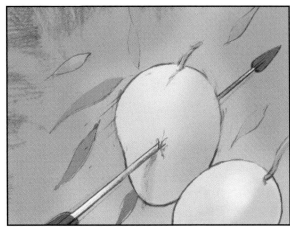

"ONE DAY, I CHANCED UPON THE PRINCES OF THE ROYAL COURT PRACTICING THEIR ARCHERY SKILLS IN THE WOODS."

"...I SPIED ON THEM FROM BEHIND THE BUSHES"

"WITH THEM WAS MY HERO - GURU DRONACHARYA. THE GOD OF ARCHERY. TRAINED BY LORD VISHNU HIMSELF."

"GURU DRONA HOVERED AROUND HIS FAVOURITE STUDENT, PRAISING HIM AND THEN GENTLY REPRIMANDING HIM."

"ARJUN, THEY CALLED HIM. THE MOST PROMISING ARCHER - ABOUT WHOM LEGENDS WOULD BE WRITTEN, THEY SAID. I DIDN'T THINK MUCH OF HIM, REALLY."

"WITH GURU DRONA HIMSELF TEACHING YOU, HOW COULD YOU NOT BE BETTER THAN THE BEST? HE LOOKED TOO SMUG ANYWAY - THE KIND OF BOY SPOILT BY LUXURY, WHO HAD NEVER HAD TO PLUCK HIS OWN BERRIES, OR KILL HIS OWN MEAT."

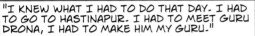

"I KNEW WHAT I HAD TO DO THAT DAY. I HAD TO GO TO HASTINAPUR. I HAD TO MEET GURU DRONA, I HAD TO MAKE HIM MY GURU."

WHAT'S THE BIG DEAL? YOU'RE TALKING ABOUT SOME TEACHER, RIGHT? YOU'RE MAKING IT SOUND LIKE A SCENE FROM THE GODFATHER!

HAVEN'T YOU EVER HAD A TEACHER YOU LOOKED UP TO? WHOSE VERY EXISTENCE WAS AN INSPIRATION? WHO TAUGHT YOU EVERYTHING YOU KNOW, ABOUT LIFE, ABOUT LEARNING ITSELF?

NOW I KNOW FOR SURE YOU NEVER DID GO TO SCHOOL... AND THE ANSWER IS NO... BUT YOU HAD ALL THAT, WITH THIS... THIS DRONA FELLOW?

NOT EXACTLY. YOU'LL UNDERSTAND WHEN I CONTINUE WITH MY STORY. MAY I?

YES.

7

THE DAYS IT TOOK ME TO REACH HASTINAPUR.

I SPENT ALL THOSE NIGHTS DREAMING ABOUT MEETING HIM. I WOULD REHEARSE WHAT I WOULD SAY TO HIM, OVER AND OVER, IN MY MIND.

I KNEW HIS TRAINING STYLE WAS TOUGH, BUT I WAS DETERMINED TO ENDURE IT – NEVER DID I THINK THAT THAT WOULD NOT BE THE TOUGHEST PART OF MY CHALLENGE.

"I WAS FINALLY GRANTED AN AUDIENCE WITH HIM. I WAS SO NERVOUS, BUT I WAS EQUALLY CONFIDENT, IN A WAY – I KNEW I HAD IT IN ME TO LEARN ARCHERY, ALL HE HAD TO DO WAS SEE ME WITH MY BOW AND ARROW, GIVE ME JUST A FEW MOMENTS OF HIS TIME... "

"BUT IT NEVER EVEN CAME TO THAT. GURU DRONA ONLY ASKED ME ONE QUESTION, AFTER HE LEARNT OF MY INTENTIONS - "

WHAT LINEAGE DO YOU BELONG TO, BOY?

"MY WORLD CAME SHATTERING DOWN. IT HAD NEVER OCCURRED TO ME THAT THE GREAT GURU WOULD STOOP SO LOW AS TO TEACH A TRIBAL BOY. IT'S EXACTLY WHAT HE SAID TO ME."

GO BACK TO YOUR TRIBE, BOY. NEVER BE SEEN AROUND HERE AGAIN.

WHAT. HAPPENED. THEN?

IT DIDN'T HAPPEN, K. I MADE IT HAPPEN.

OOH, LET ME GUESS, EK! YOU FOUND ANOTHER GURU? AND YOU ACED THAT TRAINING?

NOT EXACTLY. WHAT WOULD YOU HAVE DONE?

WHAT WOULD I HAVE DONE IF THIS HOLIER-THAN-THOU TEACHER PERSON HAD REJECTED ME?

IF YOU'D FOUND, ONE DAY, THAT EVERYTHING YOU'D BEEN HOPING FOR, DREAMING ABOUT, YOUR LIFE'S BIG AMBITION,

WHICH GAVE YOU PURPOSE AND DRIVE IN LIFE – WHICH MADE YOU WAKE UP EVERY MORNING – SNATCHED AWAY FROM YOU.

THE ONE OPPORTUNITY YOU HAD TOWARDS ACHIEVING THAT DREAM – HAD SUDDENLY, ABRUPTLY BEEN SNATCHED AWAY FROM YOU. WHAT WOULD YOU HAVE DONE?

SHEESH! YOU'RE THOSE INTENSE TYPES, HUH?

OK OK. WHAT WOULD I HAVE DONE?

YOU KNOW, IT'S EASY THESE DAYS, EK. TOO EASY. I'D SIMPLY GOOGLE IT. IN FACT, I COULD PROBABLY GOOGLE IT RIGHT NOW. GIVE ME A SECOND.

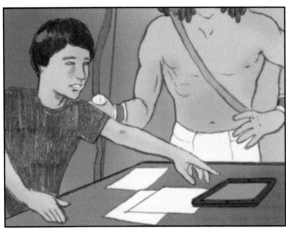

SEE FOR YOURSELF. YOUTUBE HAS TONS OF VIDEOS.

WHAT IS THIS? HOW... HOW DOES THIS... TEACH YOU?

YEAH, YOU CAN LOOK AT IT AND SEE STUFF YOU LIKE. WE DO ALL OUR SCHOOL WORK ON IT. I WAS JUST ABOUT TO FINISH THIS PROJECT ON BEES AND WHY THEY'RE DISAPPEARING - IT WAS ASSIGNED TO US THIS MORNING.

OH. REALLY? WITH THIS?

YEAH. AND YOU KNOW THE BEST PART, EK?

YOU CAN LEARN ABOUT ANYTHING YOU WANT TO LEARN?

UMM, SURE. BUT NO, I WAS GONNA SAY YOU FINISH YOUR WORK REAL QUICK.

OH!

YOU KNOW, K, I WAS THINKING, FOR A WHILE, THAT THIS... THIS BOX YOU WERE SHOWING ME WAS SIMILAR TO WHAT I DID WHEN GURU DRONA REFUSED TO HAVE ME AS HIS PUPIL.

FOR A MINUTE THERE, I THOUGHT THIS... GOOGLE, DID YOU SAY, WAS YOUR CLAY IDOL...

WHAT'S THIS CLAY IDOL BUSINESS NOW? IT'S FROM THE REST OF YOUR STORY, I'M GUESSING?

YES.

I WAS DETERMINED TO BE THE BEST ARCHER IN THE WORLD, OF ALL TIME.

"TO HAVE LEGENDS WRITTEN ABOUT ME AS MUCH AS ARJUN. MORE THAN ARJUN. SO I BUILT A SEMBLANCE OF THE GURU FROM CLAY, SET IT IN FRONT OF ME, AND BEGAN PRACTICING ARCHERY."

"I DID THIS EVERY DAY, DAY AND NIGHT, FOR DAYS AND DAYS ON END, LEARNING WITH THE CLAY MODEL IN FRONT OF ME, UNTIL I BECAME WHAT I'D SET OUT TO BECOME – I REACHED THE PINNACLE OF MY QUEST."

"I BECAME THE MASTER ARCHER TO BEAT ALL MASTER ARCHERS."

WHAT ARE YOU SAYING THEN? THAT GOOGLE CAN BE MY CLAY MODEL? WOAH, IS TECHNOLOGY MY GURU DRONA, EK?

I DON'T KNOW. CAN IT? ISN'T IT ONLY THE MEANS TO AN END - A ROUTE TO ACHIEVE YOUR DREAM, TO REALISE YOUR PASSION?

THE DRIVE, K, HAS TO BE INSIDE YOU. IT'S WHERE IT ORIGINATES FROM.

WHAT IS THIS INSIDE YOU? WHAT IS IT INSIDE ME?

IT'S CALLED MOTIVATION, K. WHAT GIVES LIFE ITS PURPOSE AND MEANING, MAKES YOU GET OUT OF BED EVERY MORNING.

YOU NEED TO UNDERSTAND IT... I WANTED TO BE THE BEST ARCHER IN THE HISTORY OF THE WORLD - THAT WAS WHAT DROVE ME - TO BE ACKNOWLEDGED IN THE OUTSIDE WORLD. THAT, AND THE YEARNING DEEP INSIDE ME TO LEARN THE SKILL, THE ART OF ARCHERY.

IF IT MEANT I HAD TO LEARN IT MYSELF, TEACH MYSELF, THEN SO BE IT.

I REALLY CAN'T SAY. I MEAN, THAT SOUNDS SO COOL - WHAT MAKES ME GET OUT OF BED EVERY MORNING.

BUT IT'S USUALLY MY ALARM CLOCK, OR MUM SCREAMING ABOUT MISSING THE BUS AGAIN, OR SOMETHING. NOTHING IMPORTANT. NOTHING SPECIAL.

THERE ALWAYS IS SOMETHING IMPORTANT AND SPECIAL, K. YOU JUST HAVEN'T RECOGNISED IT YET.

THINK ABOUT IT – WHAT IS IT INSIDE YOU THAT YOU WISH TO SEE FOR REAL IN THE REAL WORLD? WHAT KEEPS YOU AWAKE AT NIGHT? WHAT IS YOUR ULTIMATE DREAM?

WHAT REALLY MAKES YOU GET OUT OF BED, K?

K SNAPS UP AWAKE. THERE'S NO SIGN OF EK.

BUT SOMETHING'S BURNING INSIDE K. HE'S RESTLESS, HE'S THIRSTY. THE WORDS OF EK KEEP ECHOING IN HIS MIND - 'IF IT MEANT I HAD TO LEARN IT MYSELF, TEACH MYSELF, THEN SO BE IT'.

"LEARN FOR MY SELF, TEACH MY SELF – WHAT A CONCEPT! HE SIMPLY HAD TO GET TO THE BOTTOM OF THIS."

3 MONTHS AGO, IN K'S SCHOOL...

IT WAS THE FINAL STRAW IN A LONG STORY OF REJECTION AFTER FRUSTRATED REJECTION. AT FIRST, HE'D ASKED FOR AN AFTER-CLASS MEETING WITH THE ICT PROFESSOR. HE'D TOLD HIM ABOUT HIS GREAT DESIRE TO BE A GAME DESIGNER.

HOW HE'D BEEN UP NIGHTS IN A ROW, READING AND WATCHING FAMOUS GAME DESIGNERS' INTERVIEWS.

HOW HE IDOLISED SHINJI MIKAMI BECAUSE RESIDENT EVIL, EVEN ALL THESE DECADES AFTER IT CAME OUT, WAS STILL THE MOST FAR-OUT TRIP HE'D ENCOUNTERED IN THE WORLD OF GAMING.

HOW MIKAMI REVOLUTIONISED THE GENRE OF SURVIVAL HORROR GAMING WITH CONCEPTS AS ORIGINAL AS MULTIPLE ENDINGS AND AN OVER THE SHOULDER VIEWPOINT.

SHINJI MIKAMI CREATED SOMETHING TRULY INSPIRING AND CRAFTED PURE GENIUS OUT OF PUZZLES AND RIDDLES, LETHAL VIRUS STRAINS, ZOMBIE DOGS AND GIANT SPIDERS.

HIS ENTIRE GAMING PARADIGM IS A STATEMENT AGAINST CRONY CAPITALISM... THE GAME EMBODYING THE HORRORS MIKAMI GREW UP WITH IN REAL TIME, LISTENING TO STORIES ABOUT HIROSHIMA VICTIMS OF THE HOLOCAUST BEING BROUGHT TO YAMAGUCHI, WHERE MIKAMI GREW UP.

HIROSHIMA DAY IS REMEMBERED EVERY YEAR WHEN HALF A MILLION ORIGAMI CRANES LINE UP THE STREETS, IN SOLEMN MEMORY - SIGHTS MIKAMI GREW UP ON.

K HAD EXPLAINED TO HIS PROFESSOR THAT IT WASN'T JUST THE GAMING HE FOUND SO EXCITING - HE DIDN'T EVEN CONSIDER HIMSELF A "GAMER" - THOSE GUYS WERE HARD CORE, THEY WERE ADDICTED.

SURE, HE LOVED PLAYING THEM, BUT IT WAS ALWAYS CRACKING THE MIND OF THE DESIGNER, THE CREATOR, THAT KEPT HIM GOING THROUGH THE LEVELS. WHAT GOT HIM SPURRING ON, CHARGED UP WAS ALWAYS JUST THAT - IT'S WHEN HE WAS IN THE ZONE. AND HE JUST KNEW HE COULD DO IT, HE HAD IT IN HIM. BUT HE DIDN'T KNOW HOW.

WHERE DO I BEGIN?

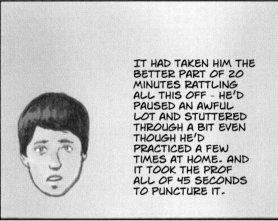

IT HAD TAKEN HIM THE BETTER PART OF 20 MINUTES RATTLING ALL THIS OFF - HE'D PAUSED AN AWFUL LOT AND STUTTERED THROUGH A BIT EVEN THOUGH HE'D PRACTICED A FEW TIMES AT HOME. AND IT TOOK THE PROF ALL OF 45 SECONDS TO PUNCTURE IT.

HE'D BEEN DULY POINTED TOWARDS THE GENERAL DIRECTION OF THE SCHOOL LIBRARY (WHERE HE FOUND ALMOST NOTHING ON GAME DESIGNING), AFTER A BARELY AUDIBLE MURMUR ABOUT HOW IT WAS "HIGH TIME HE STEPPED OUT OF THE VIRTUAL WORLD AND THOUGHT ABOUT WHAT WOULD MAKE A LIVING IN THE REAL WORLD".

HIS DAD HAD SAID A COUPLE OF WEEKS AGO...

DON'T MAKE A FOOL OF YOURSELF.

IT'S ALL BECAUSE YOU SPEND SO MUCH TIME IN CYBERSPACE...

THIS WAS ONE OF THE BIGGEST CLICHÉS HE'D ENCOUNTERED IN THE GROWN-UPS' WORLD AND HE'D NEVER UNDERSTOOD IT. THE "VIRTUAL WORLD" AS THEY CALLED IT WAS AS REAL AS THE REAL WORLD, AS FAR AS HE WAS CONCERNED.

DIDN'T THEY GET IT? JUST BECAUSE YOU TERM IT CYBERSPACE, IT DOESN'T MAKE IT ALIEN TERRITORY. WHY DOES MY DREAM TO DESIGN AND BUILD GAMES SOUND ANY LESS REAL THAN... SAY, DESIGNING BUILDINGS?

IT'S HOPELESS. WHERE DO I BEGIN?

EK, ARE YOU STILL THERE? TELL ME, REALLY - WHERE DO I BEGIN?

MAYBE HE HAS LEFT A CLUE BEHIND FOR ME!

eklavya

A NEW PAGE IS OPEN ON THE IPAD. IT IS A 1979 LETTER BY A RECORDS COMPANY ADDRESSED TO A MR. PAUL HEWSON, TELLING MR HEWSON THE RECORDING COMPANY IS NOT INTERESTED IN HIS MUSIC.

WHY DOES THAT NAME SOUND FAINTLY FAMILIAR?

3 GOOGLE SECONDS LATER

OH. BONO.

K SCROLLS THE PAGE.

COPY

WHAT! MADONNA WAS REJECTED!

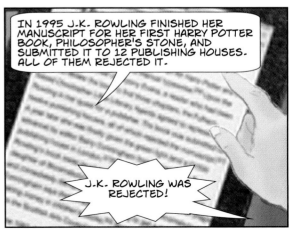

IN 1995 J.K. ROWLING FINISHED HER MANUSCRIPT FOR HER FIRST HARRY POTTER BOOK, PHILOSOPHER'S STONE, AND SUBMITTED IT TO 12 PUBLISHING HOUSES. ALL OF THEM REJECTED IT.

J.K. ROWLING WAS REJECTED!

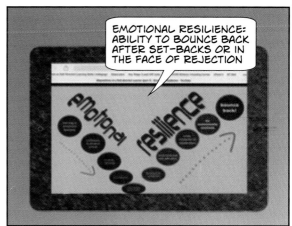

HAH! WHAT DOES IT MEAN ANYWAY? SWOT... FUNNY WORD.

IT'S AN ABBREVIATION FOR STRENGTHS, WEAKNESSES, OPPORTUNITIES & THREATS.

IT'S GENERALLY USED FOR BUSINESS ENTERPRISES BUT DAD SAYS YOU CAN APPLY IT FOR YOUR PERSONAL GROWTH ALSO, AS HE PUTS IT...

YOU'RE SUPPOSED TO LIST OUT AS MANY AS YOU CAN UNDER EACH HEADING - STRENGTHS AND WEAKNESSES ARE INTERNAL FACTORS, OPPORTUNITIES AND THREATS ARE EXTERNAL.

STRENGTHS AND OPPORTUNITIES ARE WHAT YOU NEED TO BUILD ON, AND WEAKNESSES AND THREATS ARE WHAT YOU NEED TO WORK ON.

IF YOU CAN DO THIS SYSTEMATICALLY, YOUR CHANCES AT MAXIMIZING YOUR OWN POTENTIAL AND BENEFITTING FROM IT ARE SUPER HIGH.

OR SOMETHING.

HA HA HA

ANYWAY. IT'S WHAT GOT DAD TO LAND UP AT GOOGLE, HE TELLS US.

AND THE DOWN-TIME IS WHAT KEEPS HIM THERE.

WHAT'S THAT?

ARUSHI AND SHEFALI RECOUNT...

THEIR DAD, VIKRAM, HAD EXPLAINED TO THEM...

20% TIME. THE UPSIDE OF DOWNTIME. AT GOOGLE, EMPLOYEES GET A DAY A WEEK TO DO WHAT THEY WANT TO, FOLLOW THEIR PASSIONS... DID YOU KNOW IT'S LED TO SOME OF THE BIGGEST INNOVATIONS?

A CORPORATION CALLED 3M HAS HAD THIS POLICY FOR MANY YEARS NOW AND SOME EMPLOYEES THERE CAME UP WITH THE POST-IT DURING THIS TIME. DOWNTIME.

BUT DAD! WHY WOULD ANYONE USE THE DAY OFF TO WORK?

WOULD YOU NOT JUST WANT TO LIKE, SWITCH OFF?

YES, BUT SWITCHING OFF IS A BAD THING ONLY BECAUSE YOU THINK IT MEANS WATCHING MINDLESS TV ALL DAY!

A POSITIVE SWITCHING OFF COULD GIVE YOU TIME TO FOCUS ON SOMETHING THAT'S BEEN INTRIGUING YOU BUT YOU'VE NEVER HAD THE TIME TO PURSUE.

TIME TO DAYDREAM.

DAYDREAM?! THE OTHER DAY WHEN K WAS TUNING OUT IN GEOGRAPHY, OUR TEACHER TOLD HIM TO STOP DAYDREAMING AND TO FOCUS!

'STOP BEING SO LAZY, DAYDREAMING IN THE MIDDLE OF CLASS' IS WHAT HE SAID, 'AND CONCENTRATE ON THE TASK AT HAND'.

WELL, YES, CONCENTRATING ON THE TASK AT HAND IS ESSENTIAL OF COURSE.

IT'S HOW YOU GET THINGS DONE AFTER ALL — BUT THERE'S A LOT TO BE SAID FOR CARVING A CONSCIOUS TIME OUT — IT'S PRODUCTIVE DAYDREAMING.

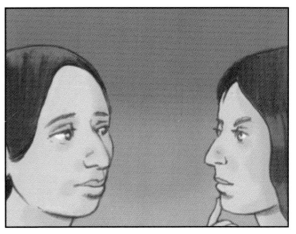

I SUPPOSE IT'S NOT FOR EVERYONE. IT'S FOR THOSE WHO CAN REMAIN FOCUSSED EVEN WHEN THERE'S A LOT GOING AROUND THEM THAT CAN DISTRACT ANYBODY... PEOPLE WITH GRIT.

GRIT? WHAT GIVES, DAD?

GRIT IS PERSEVERANCE, GIRLS. FIRM, STEADFAST PERSEVERANCE. PASSION, SUSTAINED PASSION, TO PURSUE A LONG-TERM GOAL THAT SEEMS ALMOST IMPOSSIBLE.

GRIT IS THE OPPOSITE OF BEING A DABBLER. GRIT IS NOT ABANDONING A PURSUIT BECAUSE SOMETHING NEW COMES UP, OR BECAUSE AN OBSTACLE DETERS YOU. IT'S ABOUT FOCUS. UNRELENTING FOCUS IN THE FACE OF DISTRACTION.

"THINK OF LIONEL MESSI WITH THE BALL HEADING TO THE GOAL, IRRESPECTIVE OF THE NUMBER OF TACKLERS AROUND HIM.."

"OR SACHIN TENDULKAR WHO NEVER LOSES SIGHT AS THE BOWLER RUNS UP TO THE CREASE. THAT KIND OF FOCUS IN THE FACE OF DIFFICULT CHALLENGES."

HOW ABOUT WHEN LEELA AUNTY DID THAT FRUIT AND NUTS DIET FOR RISHABH'S WEDDING? SHE REALLY STUCK TO IT AND NOTHING TEMPTED HER ALL THOSE WEEKS. IT WAS AN IMPOSSIBLE GOAL! RIGHT, DAD?

NO. THAT WOULD BE A GREAT EXAMPLE OF SELF-CONTROL. IT'S A GOOD TRAIT TO WORK ON IN LIFE. BUT GRIT IS ON ANOTHER LEVEL.

THINK OF SELF-CONTROL AS ESSENTIAL FOR A SPRINT. GRIT IS RUNNING THE MARATHON...

NOW, LET'S GET TO THAT SWOT TEST, SHALL WE?

K PICKS UP A PEN, PULLS A NOTEBOOK CLOSER AND WRITES...

K's SWOT Test

Strengths: Intelligence, Empathy.

Weaknesses: ~~Inability to find one~~ Not being able to recover from criticism.

Opportunities: Writing a school assignment like I've never done before.

Threats: Myself?

Grit = Sustained passion to pursue a <u>long-term</u>, <u>almost impossible</u> goal.

K THINKS OF THE TIME HE WENT VISITING HIS COOL COUSIN SID IN HIS HOSTEL

श्रीमद् भगवद् गीता

Srimad **Bhagavad Gita**

HOW COME YOU READ THIS EVERY DAY, SID? I MEAN, I'VE NEVER SEEN YOU READING ANY OTHER RELIGIOUS BOOK.

WHAT'S SO SPECIAL ABOUT THIS ONE?

THAT'S A GREAT QUESTION, K. YOU KNOW, THIS BOOK ISN'T SO MUCH A RELIGIOUS TEXT TO ME AS A PHILOSOPHICAL ONE. IT'S LIKE A MANUAL ON HOW TO LIVE YOUR LIFE, REALLY.

ESPECIALLY WHEN YOU'RE FACED WITH LIFE'S CHALLENGES. TIMES THAT FORCE YOU TO WONDER ABOUT THE POINT OF IT ALL.

SO YOU READ IT WHEN YOU FEEL STUCK IN LIFE?

WHEN I FEEL STUCK. WHEN I THINK THE PROBLEM IS BIGGER THAN ME. WHEN I FEEL I CAN'T GO ON.

WHEN I FEEL LIKE NO MATTER HOW MUCH OR HOW HARD I TRY, THE RESULT WILL BE A FAILURE... KNOW WHAT I MEAN?

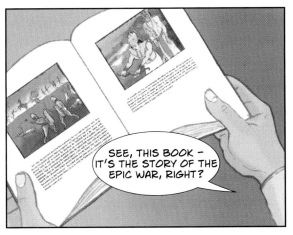

SEE, THIS BOOK – IT'S THE STORY OF THE EPIC WAR, RIGHT?

"THE WAR IS ONLY JUST AN IDEA, AN EXCUSE TO TALK ABOUT THE REALITIES OF LIFE - IT'S A GREAT EXCUSE BECAUSE WAR ESSENTIALLY MAKES YOU QUESTION EVERYTHING..."

"WHEN THE WORLD'S GREATEST ARCHER SETS DOWN HIS BOW AND FINDS HIMSELF DEFLATED AT A CRUCIAL MOMENT, QUESTIONING WHY HE'S EVEN THERE IN THE FIRST PLACE,"

"THE WORLD'S GREATEST PHILOSOPHER STEPS IN TO MAKE THINGS RIGHT."

ARJUN AND KRISHNA. YOU MEAN KRISHNA HAS THE ANSWERS OBVIOUSLY BECAUSE HE'S GOD?

NO, K- KRISHNA DOESN'T REALLY HAVE THE ANSWERS. BUT HE UNDERSTANDS LIFE AND ITS DILEMMAS, HE'S SEEN MORE OF THE WORLD, HE IS WISER THAN ARJUN.

WHAT DOES HE TELL HIM?

BASICALLY HE TELLS HIM THAT AT NO POINT IN YOUR LIFE CAN YOU EVER FORESEE THE RESULT OF YOUR ACTIONS.

AND YET ALL YOU EVER HAVE CONTROL OVER ARE YOUR ACTIONS – BECAUSE YOU'RE ALWAYS ONLY PRESENT IN THE PRESENT, NOT THE FUTURE, NOT THE PAST.

AND SO SINCE YOU ALWAYS HAVE THAT – YOUR ABILITY TO ACT – YOU SHOULD PLACE THE HIGHEST TRUST AND FAITH IN THAT AND ACT ACCORDINGLY. IT IS INFINITELY BETTER THAN OPTING FOR INACTION ANY DAY.

SID. YOU SOUND LIKE A NEW AGE-Y GURU. ONLY NOT! BUT THIS SOUNDS COOL – PLACING FAITH IN ACTION.

ONLY HOW CAN YOU NOT THINK ABOUT THE RESULTS? IF YOU'RE WORKING HARD AT SOMETHING, YOU WANT TO SUCCEED. IT'S ONLY HUMAN!

24

I USED TO FEEL THE EXACT SAME WAY, K! BUT THEN I FOUND VINDICATION IN ALL MY GODS, MY REAL RELIGIOUS TEXTS.

WHICH ARE...?

ROCK BIOGRAPHIES!

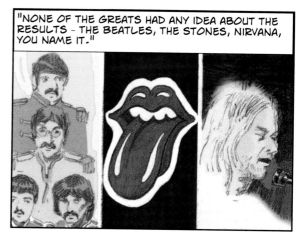

"NONE OF THE GREATS HAD ANY IDEA ABOUT THE RESULTS - THE BEATLES, THE STONES, NIRVANA, YOU NAME IT."

"THE PINK FLOYD STORY IS MY FAVOURITE. WHEN THEY STARTED THEIR 'NEW-FANGLED SHOWS' WAY BACK IN THE 70S, THERE WAS NO CONCEPT OF A MUSIC CONCERT HAVING ANYTHING OTHER THAN A BUNCH OF BOYS PLAYING DIFFERENT THINGS AND SINGING, RIGHT?"

"AND HERE COMES A BAND THAT WEAVES IN LIGHT, SOUND, LASER. AND ALL OF IT, LIVE, BABY, LIVE! THEY REDEFINED PERFORMANCE WITH THEIR HAPPENINGS AND MADE IT INTO AN ART FORM."

YEAH. BUT THAT IS COOL, SID.

NOT BACK THEN, K! THEY WERE ONLY RIDICULED FOR IT! DISMISSED AS GIMMICKS AND FLASH-IN-THE-PAN NOISE. AND LOOK WHERE THEY WENT FROM THERE.

THEY CREATED HISTORY... I THINK THEY WERE GOING WITH THE FLOW, THEY HAD FAITH IN THEIR PROCESS, THEIR IDEAS AND THEY ACTED ACCORDINGLY.

TRUST IN THE PROCESS, FAITH IN ACTION. IT'S WHAT IT'S ABOUT, K.

HOW COULD ANYONE GO ON DOING ANYTHING WHEN PEOPLE WERE MAKING FUN OF THEM, SID? I MEAN NOT THINKING ABOUT SUCCESS OR HAVING FAITH IN WHAT YOU'RE DOING IS ALL FINE

BUT YOU CAN'T BE SO CONSTRUCTIVE AND POSITIVE WHEN YOU'RE FACING RIDICULE ALL THE TIME. IT'S NOT POSSIBLE! THE PINK FLOYD GUYS MUST HAVE BEEN SUPERHEROES.

OH COME ON, K. THEY WERE JUST A BUNCH OF BOYS, JUST LIKE YOU. BUT THEY WERE HAVING FUN DOING WHAT THEY WERE DOING, ENOUGH TO NOT CARE WHAT THE STRAITJACKET MUSIC WORLD THOUGHT OF THEM.

HMM.

OR THINK OF ADELE. SHE'S CLOSER HOME FOR YOU, RIGHT? JUST A COUPLE OF YEARS OLDER.

UMM NO, SID. SHE'S CLOSER TO YOUR AGE. BUT YEAH, SHE'S ONLY A COUPLE OF DOLLARS RICHER AND PLENTY MORE FAMOUS!

WHAT ABOUT HER? SHE STRUCK GOLD AT 19, SID. I DON'T THINK SHE NEEDED TO HAVE TOO MUCH FAITH IN HER PROCESS FOR TOO LONG. IT PAID OFF PRETTY EARLY ON.

YOU KNOW HOW MUCH SHE WAS MOCKED AT FOR NOT LOOKING THE PART, K? HER BODY AND WEIGHT WERE TALKED ABOUT ALMOST AS MUCH AS HER VOICE, MAYBE MORE.

SURROUNDED AS SHE IS BY HER PEERS WHO ARE ALL OUTRAGEOUSLY SKINNY, IT'S A VERY DIFFICULT THING TO FACE, K. ESPECIALLY WHEN YOU'RE THAT YOUNG.

"IMAGINE HAVING THAT KIND OF TALENT AND THEN BEING CRITICISED FOR SOMETHING COMPLETELY IRRELEVANT – YOUR WEIGHT!"

"... BUT SHE HELD HER GROUND AND SIMPLY... SANG. 'I JUST STAND THERE AND SING', SHE TOLD THE WORLD, 'NO MATTER WHAT YOU LOOK LIKE, THE KEY IS TO BE HAPPY WITH YOURSELF'."

SHE'S BECOME A FEMINIST ICON FOR DOING THAT. BUT IT COULDN'T HAVE BEEN EASY, K. IT PROBABLY NEVER WILL BE, BECAUSE WHO KNOWS IF IT WILL EVER BE ALRIGHT FOR A WOMAN TO SAY SHE'S COMFORTABLE IN HER SKIN? BUT ADELE GOES STRONG, BECAUSE SHE TRUSTS WHAT SHE'S DOING, SHE'S DOING IT WELL, SHE'S ENJOYING IT.

IF SHE HAD STARTED FRETTING OVER BODY IMAGE ISSUES AND WHAT PEOPLE WOULD SAY, MAYBE SHE WOULD NEVER HAVE RECORDED AN ALBUM. OR SHE WOULD'VE STOPPED AFTER HER FIRST ONE... GOOD THING SHE WAS DOING IT THE GITA WAY, HUH...

HIGH TIME YOU STARTED THINKING ABOUT WHAT MAKES A LIVING IN THE REAL WORLD.

AM I GIVING UP TOO SOON?

What is important is going through with it – having faith in your effort without too much emphasis or thoughts about the results.

What you have control over is the process alone, not the end.

Work hard on it – the end is a concept lurking around the corner.

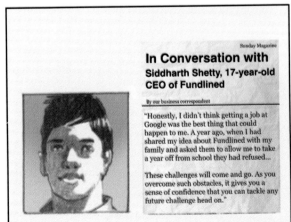

DON'T LET YOUR SUCCESSES GO TO YOUR HEAD AND YOUR FAILURES GO TO YOUR HEART.

Will Smith

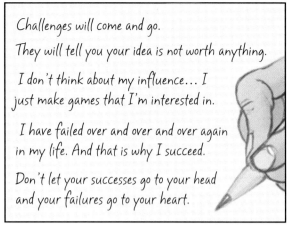

Challenges will come and go.

They will tell you your idea is not worth anything.

I don't think about my influence... I just make games that I'm interested in.

I have failed over and over and over again in my life. And that is why I succeed.

Don't let your successes go to your head and your failures go to your heart.

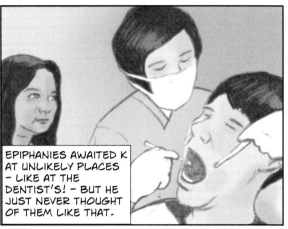

EPIPHANIES AWAITED K AT UNLIKELY PLACES - LIKE AT THE DENTIST'S! - BUT HE JUST NEVER THOUGHT OF THEM LIKE THAT.

IT'S AS IF THE MINUTE I TELL THEM WHAT I DO, THEY ALL WANT MY ADVICE ON SOMETHING OR THE OTHER THAT'S BEEN BOTHERING THEM WITH THEIR TEETH...

IT'S NOT PLEASANT TO HAVE TO PEER INTO THE INSIDES OF STRANGERS' MOUTHS, YOU KNOW, OUT OF SHEER POLITENESS.

AND JUST WHEN YOU'RE ABOUT TO TAKE A BITE OF THE LEMON TART YOURSELF!

K'S MOTHER LOVES THESE VISITS AND IF K HAD ANY ILLUSIONS ABOUT IT BEING OUT OF OVERT MATERNAL CONCERN, THEY'VE LONG BEEN DISPELLED - IT'S CLEAR SHE ACCOMPANIES HIM BECAUSE SHE ENJOYS DR. KOTECHA'S STORIES.

SHE DOES HAVE QUITE A WAY OF TELLING THEM, DON'T YOU AGREE, K?

HMM...

THE DINNER PARTY STORY IS HILARIOUS! I WONDER WHY SHE DOESN'T TELL THE GUESTS ABOUT HER OTHER PROFESSION - THAT'LL HAVE THEM STUMPED, DON'T YOU THINK?

HMM. DR. KOTECHA HAS TWO JOBS?

WELL ACTUALLY HONEY, IT'S NOT A JOB, I SHOULDN'T CALL IT HER OTHER PROFESSION. IT'S SOMETHING SHE DOES BECAUSE SHE LOVES IT SO MUCH.

WHAT IS IT, MOM?

OH HONEY, DON'T YOU REMEMBER? MAYBE YOU WERE STILL WOOZY FROM THE MEDS. SHE TOLD US THAT MONTH YOU HAD TO UNDERGO THAT EXTRACTION? SHE'S A DJ. HER SPECIALTY IS... WAIT, LET ME THINK... OH YEAH, HOUSE MUSIC.

REALLY?! A DENTIST WHO MOONLIGHTS AS A DJ! WOW! HOW DOES SHE DO THAT? WHERE'S THE TIME FOR IT? ISN'T SHE AT THE CLINIC, LIKE, EVERY DAY?

YOU KNOW, I WONDERED ABOUT THAT TOO – HOW SHE FINDS THE TIME FOR IT. I ASKED HER THE OTHER DAY AND SHE TOLD ME, QUITE MATTER-OF-FACTLY,

BUT MRS. S, THERE ARE THE WEEKENDS.

30

AND THAT MADE ME THINK — IF YOU'RE PASSIONATE ABOUT SOMETHING, YOU MAKE THE TIME. IN FACT, THEN YOU DON'T GO AROUND WITH THE EXCUSE OF NOT 'FINDING THE TIME'. IT'S ABOUT MAKING THE TIME.

DON'T YOU THINK, K?

!

ANYWAY, I'LL SUGGEST THAT THE NEXT TIME WE GO SEE HER. SHE SHOULD TELL PEOPLE AT DINNER PARTIES THAT SHE'S A DJ. THAT WAY, THE MOST SHE'LL BE ASKED TO DO IS CHANGE THE MUSIC. INFINITELY BETTER THAN BEING ASKED TO LOOK INSIDE MOUTHS, DON'T YOU THINK!

BUT MAA, WHO'S GOT THE TIME?

K MULLS OVER ALL THE TIMES HE'S USED 'LACK OF TIME' AS AN EXCUSE.

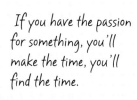

If you have the passion for something, you'll make the time, you'll find the time.

It's all about prioritizing, how you manage time - making to-do lists, sticking with them, being disciplined about them.

ANOTHER TIME, HE WAS HANGING OUT AT HIS FRIENDS' PLACE DURING THE SUMMER BREAK.

BUT THAT'S SO HIS TERRITORY, MAA.

I'M REALLY NOT INTO CRACKING THESE MIND GAMES AND ALL - WITH ALL THAT MATH IN IT. I JUST DON'T GET IT...

AND SINCE THIS IS SUPPOSED TO BE FUN, SOMETHING FUN WE'RE DOING IN OUR SUMMER HOLIDAYS.

I DON'T SEE WHY I SHOULD, IT'S NOT LIKE I PLAN ON BEING AN ACCOUNTANT!

PLEASE JUST ASK SAKSHAM. I SWEAR I'LL DO MORE ROUNDS OF WORDPOP AND EAT YOUR WORDS INSTEAD.

AND READ ANOTHER SHAKESPEARE PLAY - I CAN START ON THE TRAGEDIES THIS SUMMER - I'M ALMOST DONE READING THE COMEDIES.

MEHUL, I ALSO SAID WE'LL BE LEARNING NEW THINGS WHEN I SAID IT'LL BE SOMETHING FUN FOR THE SUMMER HOLS.

BUT I AM LEARNING NEW THINGS, AREN'T I, MAA?

I DIDN'T KNOW WHAT NEGATIVE FALLACY MEANT A FEW MONTHS AGO. SAKSHAM PROBABLY STILL THINKS IT'S SOMETHING TO DO WITH BATTERIES.

HA HA HA

GOOD POINT, MEHUL. AND SAKSHAM'S GOING TO START ON YOUR WORDY GAMES NEXT, IN FACT.

MAA, IS THIS SOME FORM OF TORTURE? PLEASE, THERE'S NO WAY I'M GOING TO PLOD THROUGH THOSE TOMES MEHUL'S ALWAYS INTO. WITH ALL THAT THOU AND THEE AND KNOWEST. HOW IS ANY OF IT RELEVANT ANYMORE?

AND I'M NOT AIMING TO BE A WRITER OR A JOURNALIST OR SOMETHING LIKE THAT. I'LL DO MORE COMPLICATED MATH GAMES, MAA. K HAS SOME, I'LL TAKE MY PEN DRIVE NEXT TIME I GO AROUND TO HIS PLACE. I'LL BE LEARNING NEW THINGS TOO.

SO LET ME GET THIS STRAIGHT.

MEHUL'S INTO BOOKS AND SAKSHAM'S INTO MATH. AND NEVER THE TWAIN SHALL MEET WITH THEIR INTERESTS?

YUP!

BUT WOULDN'T YOU WANT TO LEARN SOMETHING ABSOLUTELY NEW FROM EACH OTHER'S AREAS OF INTERESTS? DON'T YOU THINK THAT'S HOW YOUR BRAINS WOULD REALLY TRULY GROW?

BUT WHAT ABOUT INTEREST, MAA? WHY FORCE YOURSELF TO BE INTERESTED IN SOMETHING YOU'RE CLEARLY NOT?

AND NOT EVERYTHING'S MEANT FOR YOU, IS IT?

IT MAKES MORE SENSE TO BETTER YOURSELF IN THE THINGS YOU'RE NATURALLY GOOD AT, THAN TRY YOUR HAND AT EVERYTHING AND FAIL.

MORE CHANCES TO SUCCEED AS YOU GROW UP - YOU GET MORE TIME TO BETTER YOURSELF AT WHATEVER IT IS YOU'RE GOOD AT.

SURE. BUT IT'S NOT LIKE EITHER OF YOU HAVE SO MUCH AS GLANCED AT WHAT THE OTHER'S SO INTERESTED IN. IT'S LIKE YOU'VE MADE UP YOUR MINDS IT'S NOT FOR YOU.

BECAUSE WE KNOW IT IS, MAA.

OKAY. I KNOW WHAT YOU'RE SAYING - REALLY I DO. COME, TODAY, LET'S NOT GET INTO ANY OF THE NEW EXERCISES - TO DO WITH WORDS OR NUMBERS, ANYTHING MEHUL-ISH OR SAKSHAM-ISH, SO TO SPEAK.

LET'S TALK ABOUT MINDSETS INSTEAD. MAYBE IT'LL HELP CLARIFY WHERE I'M COMING FROM.

ARE YOU GOING TO TELL US ABOUT HOW WE DON'T HAVE THE RIGHT MINDSET NOW, MAA?

NOT RIGHT OR WRONG.

JUST TWO DIFFERENT KINDS OF MINDSETS. ONE IS CALLED A FIXED MINDSET AND THE OTHER'S A GROWTH MINDSET.

MINDSET IS A SIMPLE IDEA ABOUT ACHIEVEMENT AND SUCCESS.

RESEARCHED BY STANFORD PSYCHOLOGIST, CAROL DWECK.

TO PUT IT SIMPLY, PEOPLE WITH A FIXED MINDSET BELIEVE THAT INTELLIGENCE AND TALENT ARE FIXED TRAITS. IT'S LIKE 'IF YOU HAVE IT, YOU HAVE IT; IF YOU DON'T YOU DON'T.' WHAT YOU BOYS ARE SAYING ABOUT ENGLISH AND MATH, ESSENTIALLY...

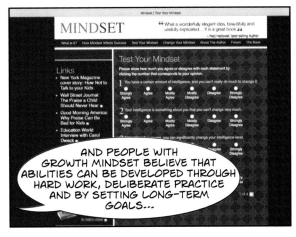

AND PEOPLE WITH GROWTH MINDSET BELIEVE THAT ABILITIES CAN BE DEVELOPED THROUGH HARD WORK, DELIBERATE PRACTICE AND BY SETTING LONG-TERM GOALS...

THE MOST IMPORTANT DIFFERENTIATING FACTOR HERE BECOMES HOW YOU FACE FAILURE – PEOPLE WITH FIXED MINDSETS DON'T ATTEMPT ANYTHING NEW FOR FEAR OF FAILING.

THEY DON'T HAVE IT IN THEM TO OVERCOME SETBACKS BECAUSE THEY STICK WITH PLAYING SAFE, THEY'RE SO AFRAID OF BEING RIDICULED.

BUT PEOPLE WITH GROWTH MINDSETS HAVE A COMPLETELY UNIQUE VIEW OF FAILURE –

THEY TREAT IT AS DATA, SOMETHING TO LEARN FROM – TO USE TO IMPROVE FUTURE PERFORMANCE...

IS IT CALLED FIXED MINDSET BECAUSE YOU'RE BORN WITH IT?

NOT AT ALL. THAT'S WHAT'S GREAT ABOUT IT. THE MINDSET ONLY REFERS TO A MINDSET AT A CERTAIN STAGE IN LIFE- IT'S NOT LIKE A GENETIC DISEASE OR SOMETHING!

YOU CAN WORK ON FIXING YOUR FIXED MINDSET, IN OTHER WORDS. WORK ON EVOLVING IT INTO A GROWTH MINDSET, AS YOU GROW. IT'LL SERVE YOU WELL IN LIFE.

HERE, TAKE THE MINDSET QUIZ.

K TAKES THE MINDSET QUIZ.

K DOESN'T EVEN KNOW WHEN THE DAY TURNS INTO DUSK & DUSK INTO MIDNIGHT. WHEN HE OPENS HIS EYES, HE CAN'T BELIEVE IT.

HE WASN'T ASLEEP AND YET HE WAS NOT AWAKE. HE WAS... THINKING, HE COULD SAY, AT BEST. HE CAN'T THINK OF A TIME IN HIS LIFE HE'S SPENT IN DEEP THOUGHT LIKE THAT. IT FELT LIKE... MEDITATION. OR WHAT THEY SAY ABOUT IT, IN ANY CASE. HE DIDN'T SO MUCH AS EVEN LOOK AT HIS PHONE DURING THAT TIME, DIDN'T CHECK HIS FACEBOOK, DIDN'T TOUCH THE MAC, DID NOT EVEN GAME.

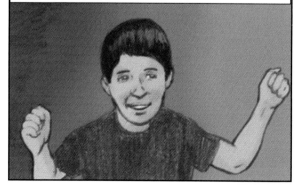

THIS HAS NEVER HAPPENED TO K BEFORE. EVER. AND HE FEELS ENERGIZED. ENTHUSED. WHAT DOES THIS MEAN?

Resources

Videos on dispositions of a self-directed learner:

- Intrinsic Motivation: http://youtu.be/QZxh5ax-HoE

- Self-Control and Delayed Gratification: http://youtu.be/74O5SYcLqVg

- Grit: http://youtu.be/nCNsiPB5sJ8

- Attention Management: http://youtu.be/7a2AVbW3AkA

- Self-Efficacy: http://youtu.be/lXyl8iDmRbU

- Growth Mindset: http://youtu.be/htXA-bIbUU0

- Emotional Resilience: http://youtu.be/w8i3Gn0mEnE

- Curiosity: http://youtu.be/BKLf44bPMkw

   (these above videos can be accessed on our YouTube Channel

   http://youtube.com/timelesslifeskills)

- Dan Pink - The Puzzle of Motivation: http://youtu.be/rrkrvAUbU9Y

- Walter Mischel - Marshmallow study and Self-Control - http://vimeo.com/109065003

- Angela Lee Duckworth: The Key to Success? Grit - http://youtu.be/H14bBuluwB8

- Carol Dweck on Mindset - http://youtu.be/QGvR_0mNpWM

- Ellen Langer on Paying Attention - http://youtu.be/cz94BmOIroA

- Switch, a book on Behavioural Change: http://youtu.be/qmmwWxVzSsw

Videos on the changing 21st century context:

- Life Skills for Success and Well-being in the 21st century - http://youtu.be/A1k-4pqAuXA

- Humans Need Not Apply: www.youtube.com/watch?v=7Pq-S557XQU

ESSENTIAL DISPOSITIONS OF AN INSPIRED LEARNER

K FOUND INSPIRATION IN A CHANCE ENCOUNTER WITH EKLAVYA, WHICH SET HIM
ON AN INNER JOURNEY OF REFLECTION - A JOURNEY THAT THEN BROUGHT HIM
CLOSER TO UNDERSTANDING LEARNING FOR ITS OWN SAKE.
YOU TOO CAN EMBARK ON THIS JOURNEY, IN FACT WE URGE YOU TO.

INTRINSIC MOTIVATION
INSTEAD OF THE LURE OF REWARDS
OR FEAR OF PUNISHMENT, YOU ARE
DRIVEN BY PURSUIT OF AUTONOMY,
MASTERY AND PURPOSE.

GROWTH MINDSET
WHEN YOU BELIEVE THAT TRAITS
CAN BE CULTIVATED THROUGH
YEARS OF PASSION, TOIL AND
TRAINING, AND ARE NOT SIMPLY
WHAT YOU'RE BORN WITH.

EMOTIONAL RESILIENCE
THE ABILITY TO BOUNCE BACK AFTER
A SETBACK, AND NOT BE DOWN AND
OUT AFTER THE FIRST FALL!

GRIT
TENACIOUS, DOGGED
DETERMINATION TO PURSUE
LONG-TERM, ALMOST
IMPOSSIBLE GOALS, DESPITE
BOREDOM, DISAPPOINTMENT,
FRUSTRATION AND SETBACKS.

SELF-CONTROL, ABILITY TO DELAY GRATIFICATION
YOU ARE ABLE TO FOREGO THE IMMEDIATE SMALLER BENEFIT FOR A FUTURE
LARGER BENEFIT, AND REALLY BE ABLE TO MAKE THAT DISTINCTION FOR YOURSELF.

K'S MANTRAS

WHAT YOU HAVE CONTROL OVER IS THE PROCESS
ALONE, NOT THE END. PUT IN THE WORK - THE END
IS A CONCEPT LURKING AROUND THE CORNER.

MAKE TIME FOR WHAT YOU WANT TO DO.

WHAT MAKES YOU GET OUT BED
EACH DAY? IF YOU CAN ANSWER
THAT QUESTION TRUTHFULLY,
THEN PURSUING WHAT IT IS,
IS ALL THAT MATTERS.

TURN WHAT DRIVES YOU INTO
WHAT DRIVES YOUR LEARNING.

WHEN YOU FIND YOUR PASSION,
NURTURE IT. STICK WITH IT, WORK
ON IT, MAKE TIME FOR IT, AND YOU
WILL SEE IT BLOOM.

LEARNING = GROWING = FLOURISHING.

YOUR DREAM IS REAL. NOW PLAN THE INCEPTION.

WE ARE GRATEFUL

THIS COMIC EBOOK WAS MADE POSSIBLE BECAUSE OF THE GENEROUS CONTRIBUTION MADE BY THESE FOLKS AT OUR CROWD FUNDING CAMPAIGN. WE ARE INDEBTED TO THEM.

AHAANA

AL BEARD

ANDREW & SARAH

DIMPLE AGARWAL

DIVYA GURURAJ

EDWARDIAN GROUP LONDON

ELLA VALA

GAURAV SETHI

GAUTAM SINGH DEO

HARISH KOTECHA

JAGDISH & KUSUM PANT

JAGRAVI UPADHYAY

LIZ FASCINA

MANAN

MAPLE CAPITAL ADVISORS

MARK LEWIN

MILAN CHAUHAN

NEETI AWASTHI

NIHAR DAS

NILIMA SHAH

NISHMA GOSRANI

PARESH SHAH

RAJEEV JOSHI

RICHARD KELSEY

RAVI SHAH

RAYHAAN HASSIM

SABITA GUPTA

SACHIN GUPTA

SACHIN UTTAM

SANJAY MALAVIYA

SANVALI KAUSHIK

SARITA KOTECHA

SHANKAR SHARMA

SHAYASTA ASHIQ

SUNDER NARAYANA

SUNNY NARANG

SUSHIL RADIA

SWATI & SUYASH

VANDITA PANT

VIKRAM SAHAI

 ABOUT TIMELESS LIFESKILLS

WE ARE A LONDON-BASED SOCIAL-ENTERPRISE ADDRESSING THREE KEY ISSUES - RELEVANT CURRICULUM (LIFE SKILLS NEEDED FOR FLOURISHING IN THE 21ST CENTURY), ENTICING LEARNING EXPERIENCE (THAT APPEALS TO TODAY'S DISTRACTED LEARNERS) AND AFFORDABILITY (TO MAKE EDUCATION INCLUSIVE AS IT IS OTHERWISE BECOMING EXPENSIVE AND HENCE EXCLUSIVE).

TOWARDS THIS WE ARE BUILDING AN ONLINE LEARNING ACADEMY THAT OFFERS INNOVATIVE LEARNING SOLUTIONS TO IMPART SKILLS ESSENTIAL FOR SUCCESS AND WELL-BEING. WE PLAN TO BRING OUT MORE COMIC BOOKS, INTERACTIVE STORIES, APPS, GAMES, COURSES AND CONDUCT MORE WORKSHOPS.

1,000 COPIES OF THE ADVENTURES OF K, IN ITS HINDI VERSION, IS GOING OUT TO 200 SCHOOLS FOR THE UNDERPRIVILEGED ACROSS INDIA FOR FREE. WE HAVE MADE THIS COMIC AVAILABLE ON PWYW (PAY WHAT YOU WANT) BASIS. WE SUCCESSFULLY PILOTED A 6-WEEK ONLINE COURSE ON SELF-DIRECTED LEARNING SKILLS IN OCTOBER 2014 WITH 100 STUDENTS. WE PLAN TO OFFER THIS COURSE ON A REGULAR BASIS AND ADD MORE ONLINE COURSES.

LET'S DO MORE EPIC STUFF TOGETHER! PLEASE GET IN TOUCH IF YOU NEED ANY INFORMATION OR WOULD LIKE TO EXPLORE SYNERGIES:

WEBSITE: WWW.TIMELESSLIFESKILLS.CO.UK ; EMAIL: INFO@TIMELESSLIFESKILLS.CO.UK
FOLLOW US ON FACEBOOK: WWW.FACEBOOK.COM/LIFESKILLS

YOU CAN DOWNLOAD THIS COMIC IN EBOOK FORMAT, FOR FREE OR AT A PRICE OF YOUR CHOICE, AT HTTP://GUM.CO/YEARNINGFORLEARNING

YOU CAN DOWNLOAD THE HINDI TRANSLATION OF THIS COMIC, IN EBOOK FORMAT, FOR FREE OR AT A PRICE OF YOUR CHOICE, AT HTTP://GUM.CO/TADAP